ANDREA DAVIS PINKNEY

Dear Benjamin Banneker

Illustrated by
BRIAN PINKNEY

GULLIVER BOOKS
HARCOURT BRACE & COMPANY
San Diego   New York   London

Text copyright © 1994 by Andrea Davis Pinkney
Illustrations copyright © 1994 by Brian Pinkney

Library of Congress Cataloging-in-Publication Data
Pinkney, Andrea Davis.
Dear Benjamin Banneker/Andrea Davis Pinkney;
illustrated by Brian Pinkney.
p. cm.
"Gulliver books."
ISBN 0-15-200417-3
1. Banneker, Benjamin, 1731—1806—Juvenile literature.
2. Almanacs, American—History—Juvenile literature.
[1. Banneker, Benjamin, 1731—1806. 2. Astronomers. 3. Almanacs—History.
4. Afro—Americans—Biography.] I. Pinkney, Brian, ill. II. Title.
QB143.B35P56 1994 520'.92—dc20 93-31162 [B]

First edition   A B C D E

The illustrations in this book were prepared as scratchboard rendering,
hand-colored with oil paint. The display type was set in Pabst Oldstyle No. 45
and the text type was set in Caslon Old Face by the Photocomposition Center,
Harcourt Brace & Company, San Diego, California.
Color separations by Bright Arts, Ltd., Singapore
Production supervision by Warren Wallerstein and David Hough
Designed by Trina Stahl and Lori J. McThomas

PRINTED IN SINGAPORE

Special thanks to Silvio A. Bedini for his extensive research and writing on the life of Benjamin Banneker. Also, appreciation goes to the Banneker-Douglass Museum and The Friends of Benjamin Banneker Historical Park for the preservation of Benjamin Banneker's legacy.

—A. D. P. & B. P.

To my brother, P. J.
   —A. D. P.

To my mother and father
   —B. P.

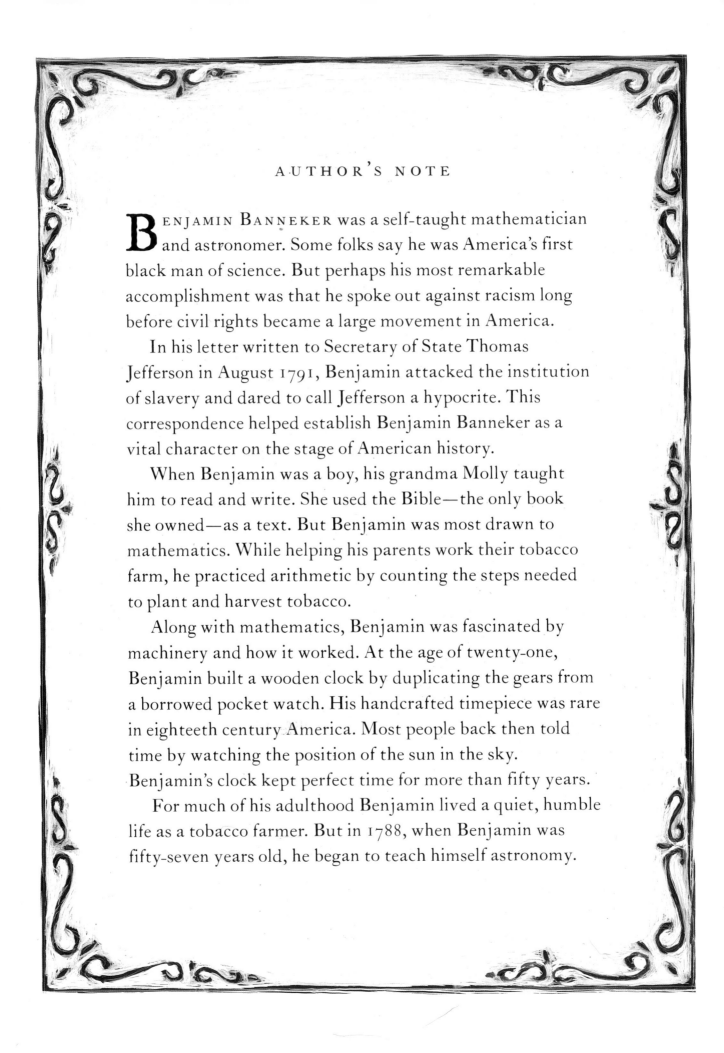

AUTHOR'S NOTE

BENJAMIN BANNEKER was a self-taught mathematician and astronomer. Some folks say he was America's first black man of science. But perhaps his most remarkable accomplishment was that he spoke out against racism long before civil rights became a large movement in America.

In his letter written to Secretary of State Thomas Jefferson in August 1791, Benjamin attacked the institution of slavery and dared to call Jefferson a hypocrite. This correspondence helped establish Benjamin Banneker as a vital character on the stage of American history.

When Benjamin was a boy, his grandma Molly taught him to read and write. She used the Bible—the only book she owned—as a text. But Benjamin was most drawn to mathematics. While helping his parents work their tobacco farm, he practiced arithmetic by counting the steps needed to plant and harvest tobacco.

Along with mathematics, Benjamin was fascinated by machinery and how it worked. At the age of twenty-one, Benjamin built a wooden clock by duplicating the gears from a borrowed pocket watch. His handcrafted timepiece was rare in eighteeth century America. Most people back then told time by watching the position of the sun in the sky. Benjamin's clock kept perfect time for more than fifty years.

For much of his adulthood Benjamin lived a quiet, humble life as a tobacco farmer. But in 1788, when Benjamin was fifty-seven years old, he began to teach himself astronomy.

Through his studies of astronomy, Benjamin learned to predict the weather. He even predicted an eclipse of the sun. An accomplished scientist, Benjamin used his skills to create an almanac — something no black man had ever done before.

In January 1791, President George Washington and Secretary of State Thomas Jefferson hired Benjamin to help survey a new nation's capital, which was later named Washington, D.C. Benjamin worked alongside Major Andrew Ellicott IV, one of the finest surveyors in the United States. Using the stars as his guide, Benjamin helped Ellicott lay the city's boundaries.

Like many trailblazers, Benjamin stood up for what he thought was right, and spoke out against what he believed to be wrong. It took almost 100 years for slaves to be granted their freedom from the time Benjamin wrote to Thomas Jefferson, voicing his views on the injustices of slavery.

Yet Benjamin Banneker, one of the first black men in American history to correspond with a government official, was brave enough to challenge the secretary of state to live up to the ideal Jefferson promised when he wrote the Declaration of Independence in 1776: "life, liberty and the pursuit of happiness" for everyone.

ANDREA DAVIS PINKNEY

NO SLAVE MASTER ever ruled over Benjamin
Banneker as he was growing up in Maryland
along the Patapsco River. He was as free as the sky
was wide, free to count the slugs that made their
home on his parents' tobacco farm, free to read, and
to wonder: *Why do the stars change their place in the sky
from night to night? What makes the moon shine full, then,
weeks later, disappear? How does the sun know to rise just
before the day?*

Benjamin's mother, Mary, grew up a free woman. His daddy, Robert, a former slave, gained his freedom long before 1731 when Benjamin was born. Benjamin Banneker had official papers that spelled out his freedom.

But even as a free person, Benjamin had to work hard. When Benjamin grew to be a man, he discovered that to earn a decent living he had little choice but to tend to the tobacco farm his parents left him, a grassy hundred acres he called Stout.

Benjamin worked long hours to make sure his farm would yield healthy crops. After each harvest, Benjamin hauled hogshead bundles of tobacco to sell in town. The work was grueling and didn't leave him much time for finding the answers to his questions about the mysterious movements of the stars and cycles of the moon.

But over the course of many years, Benjamin managed to teach himself astronomy at night while everyone else slept.

There were many white scientists in Benjamin's day who taught themselves astronomy and published their own almanacs. But it didn't occur to them that a black man—free or slave—could be smart enough to calculate the movements of the stars the way Benjamin did.

Benjamin wanted to prove folks wrong. He knew that he could make an almanac as good as any white scientist's. Even if it meant he would have to stay awake most nights to do it, Benjamin was determined to create an almanac that would be the first of its kind.

In colonial times, most families in America owned an almanac. To some, it was as important as the Bible. Folks read almanacs to find out when the sun and moon would rise and set, when eclipses would occur, and how the weather would change from season to season. Farmers read their almanacs so they would know when to seed their soil, when to plow, and when they could expect rain to water their crops.

Beginning in 1789, Benjamin spent close to a year observing the sky every night, unraveling its mysteries. He plotted the cycles of the moon and made careful notes.

The winter of 1790 was coming. In order to get his
almanac printed in time for the new year, Benjamin
needed to find a publisher quickly. He sent his
calculations off to William Goddard, one of the most
well-known printers in Baltimore. William Goddard
sent word that he wasn't interested in publishing
Benjamin's manuscript. Benjamin received the same
reply from John Hayes, a newspaper publisher.

Benjamin couldn't find a publisher who was willing to take a chance on him. None seemed to trust his abilities. Peering through his cabin window at the bleak wintry sky, Benjamin's own faith in his almanac began to shrivel, like the logs burning in his fireplace.

Finally, in late 1790, James Pemberton learned of Benjamin Banneker and his almanac. Pemberton was the president of the Pennsylvania Society for the Abolition of Slavery, a group of men and women who fought for the rights of black people. Pemberton said Benjamin's almanac was proof that black people were as smart as white people. He set out to help Benjamin get his almanac published for the year 1791.

With Pemberton's help, news about Benjamin and his almanac spread across the Maryland countryside and up through the channels of the Chesapeake Bay. Members of the abolitionist societies of Pennsylvania and Maryland rallied to get Benjamin's almanac published.

But as the gray days of December grew shorter and colder, Benjamin and his supporters realized it was too late in the year 1790 to publish Benjamin's astronomy tables for 1791. Benjamin would have to create a new set of calculations for an almanac to be published in 1792.

Benjamin knew many people would use and learn
from his almanac. He also realized that as the first
black man to complete such a work, he'd receive
praise for his accomplishment. Yet, Benjamin
wondered, what good would his almanac be to black
people who were enslaved? There were so many black
people who wouldn't be able to read his almanac.
Some couldn't read and were forbidden to learn.
Others, who could read, had masters who refused to
let them have books. These thoughts were never far
from Benjamin's mind as he worked on his 1792
almanac.

Once his almanac was written, Benjamin realized he had another task to begin. On the evening of August 19, 1791, Benjamin lit a candle and sat down to write an important letter to Secretary of State Thomas Jefferson. The letter began:

Maryland, Baltimore County,
Near Ellicott's Lower Mills August 19th. 1791.
Thomas Jefferson Secretary of State.

Sir, I am fully sensible of the greatness of that freedom which I take with you on the present occasion; a liberty which Seemed to me Scarcely allowable, when I reflected on the distinguished, and dignifyed station in which you Stand; and the almost general prejudice and prepossession which is so previlent in the world against those of my complexion.

Years before, in 1776, Thomas Jefferson wrote the Declaration of Independence, a document that said "all men are created equal." But Thomas Jefferson owned slaves. How, Benjamin wondered, could Thomas Jefferson sign his name to the declaration, which guaranteed "life, liberty and the pursuit of happiness" for all? The words Thomas Jefferson wrote didn't match the way he lived his life. To Benjamin, that didn't seem right.

Benjamin knew that all black people could study
and learn as he had—if only they were free to do so.
Written on the finest paper he could find, Benjamin's
letter to Thomas Jefferson said just that. His letter
reminded Thomas Jefferson that before he came
to the United States from England, he—a white
man—had been a slave under British rule. He went
on to say:

> *Sir how pitiable is it to reflect, that altho you were so*
> *fully convinced of the benevolence of the Father of*
> *mankind, and of his equal and impartial distribution of*
> *those rights and privileges which he had conferred upon*
> *them, that you should at the Same time counteract his*
> *mercies, in detaining by fraud and violence so numerous*
> *a part of my bretheren under groaning captivity and cruel*
> *oppression, that you should at the Same time be found*
> *guilty of that most criminal act, which you professedly*
> *detested in others, with respect to yourselves.*

Along with his letter, Benjamin enclosed a copy of
his almanac.

Eleven days later, Benjamin received a reply from Thomas Jefferson. In his letter, Jefferson wrote that he was glad to get the almanac and that he agreed with Benjamin, black people had abilities that they couldn't discover because they were enslaved. He wrote:

Philadelphia, Aug. 30. 1791.

Sir, I Thank you sincerely for your letter of the 19th instant and for the Almanac it contained. No body wishes more than I do to see such proofs as you exhibit, that nature has given to our black brethren, talents equal to those of the other colors of men, and that the appearance of a want of them is owing merely to the degraded condition of their existence. . . .

Jefferson wrote Benjamin that he wanted things to change. He hoped, in time, that black people would be treated better. He said:

I can add with truth, that no body wishes more ardently to see a good system commenced for raising the condition both of their body & mind to what it ought to be, as fast as the imbecility of their present existence, and other circumstances which cannot be neglected, will admit.

Benjamin reread the secretary of state's letter
several times. Then he folded it carefully and tucked
it in one of his astronomy books for safekeeping.
Benjamin had spoken his mind in the hope that all
people would someday be free.

In December 1791, store owners started selling
Benjamin Banneker's Pennsylvania, Maryland,
Delaware, and Virginia almanac for the year 1792.
Townsfolk from near and far purchased the book.
The first edition sold out right away.

Benjamin's almanac contained answers to some of the questions he had asked himself when he was a boy watching the sky. It included cycles of full moons and new moons, times of sunrise and sunset, tide tables for the Chesapeake Bay, and news about festivals and horse habits.

The success of Benjamin's almanac meant that he was free to leave tobacco farming behind. Benjamin sold most of his land but kept his cabin so that he could spend the rest of his days studying astronomy, asking more questions, and finding the answers.

Benjamin published an almanac every year until
1797. His 1793 almanac included the letter he had
written to Thomas Jefferson, along with the
secretary of state's reply.

Benjamin didn't live to see the day when black
people were given their freedom. But his almanacs
and the letter he wrote to Thomas Jefferson showed
everybody that all men are indeed created equal.